100

Fun and Fabulous Ways to

Flirt with Your Spouse

Doug Fields

Artwork by Marian Nixon

HARVEST HOUSE PUBLISHERS
EUGENE, OREGON

100 Fun and Fabulous Ways to Flirt with Your Spouse

Text Copyright © 2000 by Doug Fields
Published by Harvest House Publishers
Eugene, Oregon 97402

ISBN 0-7369-0390-9

Text is adapted from *Creative Romance* by
Doug Fields (Harvest House Publishers, 1991).

Marian Nixon
2867 West Leland Avenue, #3
Chicago, IL 60625
(773) 588-8640

Design and production by Garborg Design Works, Minneapolis, Minnesota

Scripture quotations are taken from: The Living Bible, Copyright © 1971 owned by assignment by Illinois Bank N.A. (as trustee). Used by permission of Tyndale House Publishers, Inc., Wheaton, Illinois 60189. All rights reserved; and from the Holy Bible, New International Version ®, Copyright © 1973, 1978, 1984 by the International Bible Society. Used by permission of Zondervan Publishing House.

Printed in China.

06 07 08 09 / PP / 10 9 8 7 6 5

Creative Romance

Flirting with your spouse is a concept whose time has come! And it certainly doesn't take a Caribbean cruise to put that sparkle in your loved one's eyes. Simple gestures—writing "I Love You" across the lawn, filling her sink with flowers, snuggling down with him in front of the fire—can keep a relationship fun and exciting. These 100 fabulous ideas provide many romantic moments for you and your honey to share and remember.

Have a great time!

1

Establish a date-night once a week. This planned-for time of shared experience and intimacy brings you closer together.

2

Write a love story of how you met and get it printed and bound.

4

I have found the one
whom my soul loves.

The Song of Songs

Rent a classic love-story video and watch it while cuddling under blankets.

 Whisper something romantic to your spouse in a crowded room.

5 Let your husband know that you respect him. Encourage him for being romantic. Catch him doing things right in his role as a husband.

Make up nicknames for each other.

7 Look for ways to encourage your wife. Don't let the little things go unnoticed. Encourage her beauty, her thoughts, her feelings, actions, and opinions.

Mail a love letter to your spouse's place of work.

9 Insert the word "attention" into your attitude vocabulary. Make sure your spouse feels she gets your full focus and consideration.

10 Decide not to go to a social event at the last minute and instead go somewhere alone.

11

Write a poem for
your spouse.

12 Plan to get up some morning and head
out in the car with the absolute determi-
nation that you aren't going to plan one
single thing. Just drive north, south, east, or west,
and stop when you feel like it. Look in a shop or at
a garage sale, take a picture, or go for a walk on a
pier. Go wherever you feel like going, discover new
territory, and explore unknown spots.

13

Be generous with compliments.

All beautiful you are, my darling;
there is no flaw in you.

The Song of Songs

12

Take your spouse to one of your favorite restaurants from your "dating days." Order something indulgent and reminisce about falling in love.

Take a horse-drawn carriage ride.

16.

Sketch your dream house floor plan together and talk about the possibilities for each room.

17

Give him a back rub.

18

Surprise your spouse by making a fire in the fireplace instead of going to bed. Serve your favorite ice cream as you sit and talk in front of the fire.

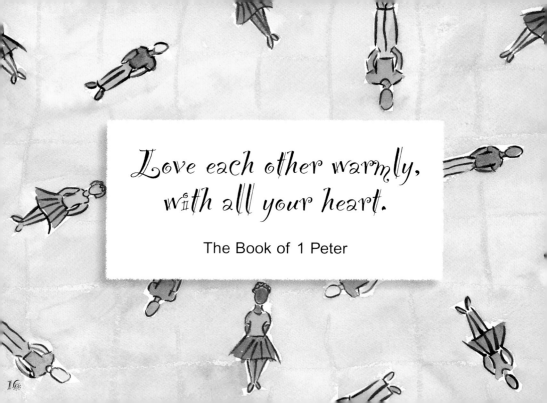

Love each other warmly,
with all your heart.

The Book of 1 Peter

19 Picnic by a pond.

20 ☆ If you are going to be away from home for a significant amount of time, find ways to show your love from a distance. One easy way is to leave notes, cards, recorded messages, flowers, and other personalized gifts around the house in places where they are sure to be discovered. You can also ask friends to help you deliver surprises every day you are absent.

 21 Develop a weekly dining spot to meet for lunch.

 22 Reserve a room for one night at a local hotel without your spouse's knowledge. Tell him you would like to go to dinner at the hotel's restaurant. Check in and get the key without letting him know. After eating, browse through the lobby and the shops. Suggest a romantic ride in the elevator. When the elevator stops at your floor, surprise him by escorting him to your "love suite."

 Give your mate a foot massage.

24

Put on your spouse's favorite romantic music and take her dancing around your candlelit living room.

25 Remember to look into your spouse's eyes while she tells you about her day.

 26

Take your spouse on a "local vacation." Pretend to be tourists and visit some of the sights in your own town that you've never experienced. End by having dinner at a new restaurant.

27 Write out 50 reasons you're glad to be married.

28

Your spouse is worthy of your generous approval. Be lavish with your loving words.

29

Set candles above the bed.

30 Nothing would please (and surprise) your spouse more than reading the morning paper and finding a professional ad with a love note from you. Placing an ad in the local paper is an easy way to say "I love you," and it will stick in his memory longer than the sports page headlines.

31

Read to one another in bed.

32

Put perfume on your bed sheets.

Hug your husband from behind and give him a kiss on the back of the neck.

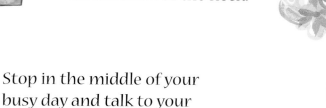

Stop in the middle of your busy day and talk to your spouse for 15 minutes about how much he or she means to you.

35

Create your own special holiday.

36

On little notes write romantic words
from the dictionary and leave them
in places your spouse will find them.

Swing in a
hammock together.

While driving, pull over for scenic sights
and get out of the car together to take
in the panoramic beauty.

39

Mail your spouse love letters instead
of leaving them in the house.

40

Spend time putting together
a puzzle on a rainy night.

41 Make heart-shaped pancakes and serve them in bed.

You have stolen my heart. . .

The Song of Songs

42 Tell your spouse "I'd rather be here with you right now than any place else in the world."

 43 Brush her hair.

44 Take time to think about him during the day, then tell him what you thought.

45 Encourage your spouse to share with you her dreams. Take the time to ask questions that show her you are interested in wishes she holds in her heart.

Be creative in thinking
of ways to make your
spouse laugh.

47 Study your monthly calendar and
choose at least two days on which
you can schedule something spe-
cial for your mate. When they arrive, go out of
your way to communicate your love.

48 Reminisce about your first kiss or your first date.

49 Take a small camera with you whenever you go on a date. In doing so, you'll find it easy to maintain and document great moments to remember.

50

Take time to watch the sun come up or go down together.

51

Designate different locations where you've had great experiences as your personal "special spots." That will make a simple walk through your special park an incredible gesture of love.

52

Go on a walk and
pick flowers.

53

Attach a city or area map to a wall and
highlight different areas that would be a
fun site for a date. After blindfolding and
spinning your wife around a few times, have her walk
to the map and stick a pin in a section of the map. Take
her to the spot closest to where she placed the pin.

54

Snuggle down together on the sofa and reminisce through old photo albums.

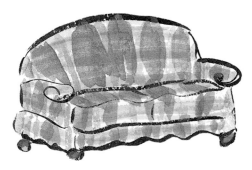

55

Make your spouse feel special by surprising him or her with a gift. Once you've decided on the "right" gift to buy, think of some unique ways to present it to your husband or wife.

56 Serve your spouse breakfast in bed.

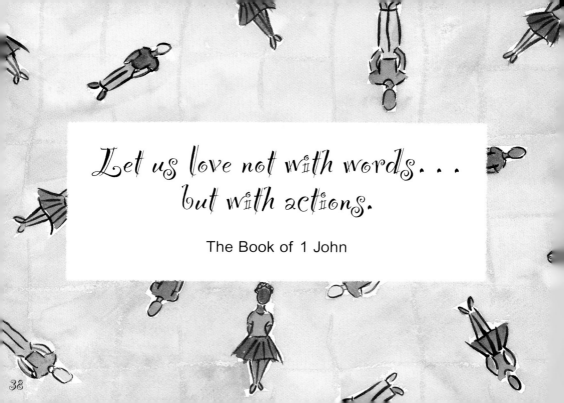

Let us love not with words. . .
but with actions.

The Book of 1 John

57 Set up a bed of comfort for your wife. Serve her a refreshing beverage, fan her toward a restful mood, and hand feed her grapes or exotic fruits.

58 Place a rose on her pillow.

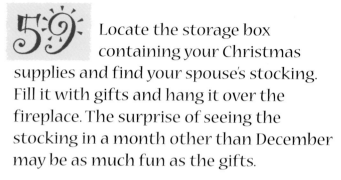 Locate the storage box containing your Christmas supplies and find your spouse's stocking. Fill it with gifts and hang it over the fireplace. The surprise of seeing the stocking in a month other than December may be as much fun as the gifts.

Dedicate a song to her over the radio.

Place a gift in the bottom of your husband's favorite box of cereal. Act surprised when your small, wrapped present plops into his bowl.

Wink and smile at your spouse from across the room.

63 Combine romance with learning something new together to create a great lesson in love. You can sign up for a weekend retreat throwing pottery, tackling conversational Japanese, exploring astronomy, or considering the migration of the California gray whale.

64 Fill the freezer with his favorite desserts.

65 Whether it's for a weekend or a weeklong vacation, take your spouse on a bicycle tour through scenic countryside. Add to your memories by stopping along the way at romantic country inns.

66 List your spouse's best qualities in alphabetical order.

Surprise your spouse with a one-night vacation by renting a cabin with a fireplace. Unplug the phone, the TV, and the radio. Fall asleep together in front of the fire.

 Serve your spouse milk and cookies in bed.

There are few things more rewarding
than verbal appreciation from a
spouse. Take time to let you husband
know how much you value him.

Design a date especially suited to
your wife's personality.

Being liberal with praise doesn't have to happen only behind closed doors. When you compliment your husband or wife in the presence of others, it amounts to a double blessing.

72 Tell your husband, "I thought about you all day and couldn't wait to see you!"

73 Surprise your mate by placing an encouraging note in her pocket before she leaves for work. By leaving notes in the pockets of pants, jackets, blouses, and sweaters, you'll condition your spouse to become a "pocket searcher" for your kind words.

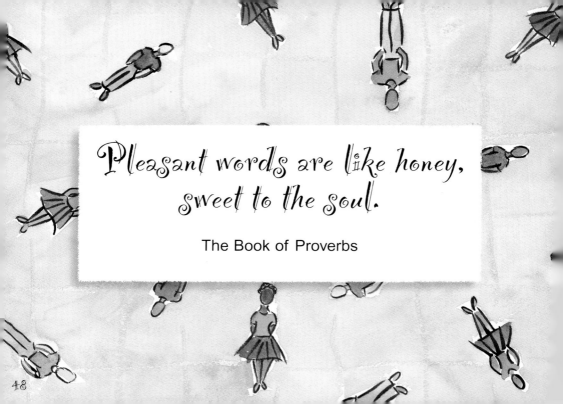

Pleasant words are like honey,
sweet to the soul.

The Book of Proverbs

48

74 Call your husband during the day and remind him of your love for him.

75 Use your answering machine as a way to leave romantic messages expressing your love for your spouse.

76 Use your video camera to interview some of the people closest to your husband. Record them as they tell you what they like most about your mate. Surprise your husband by putting in your homemade video when he's expecting the next rental movie.

77 Stand together in front of a lake and watch your reflections.

 78

Celebrate for no reason.

79 Warmly acknowledge the little changes your spouse makes to his or her appearance.

80

Frequently remember to tell your
husband or wife "I love you because…"

81

Do something your spouse loves to do,
even though it doesn't interest you
personally.

Let love be your greatest aim.

The Book of 1 Corinthians

Remember something she thinks you've forgotten.

Have a hot bubble bath ready for her when she comes home after the end of a long day.

84 Use a tender touch as you pass one another around the house.

85 Read a loving passage about your spouse from your journal.

Hold hands.

Bring home flowers.

 Surprise your spouse with an ice-cold drink while he or she is working hard on a hot day.

 Rub feet under the table.

Break away from the chaos of the
family long enough to share an
intimate conversation.

Kiss your spouse's fingers.

Leave a photo of yourself
on his dashboard.

 Plant a tree
together in honor
of your marriage.

94 Be attentive to the likes and dislikes of your spouse that are casually communicated through everyday conversation. Surprise him or her with little gifts that show how well you listened.

 95

Surprise her by filling her bathroom sink with fresh flowers.

Make time for your spouse. Show him that he is
worth your undivided attention.

Initiate laughter by playing fun, loving, and creative practical jokes on each other.

Have a candlelit picnic
in the backyard.

99 When time is short, be creative about "minidates." Get outside the house and invest a few minutes in each other. If you initiate the desire to be alone together during a busy time you will score big points in the thoughtful-category.

Say often, "I'd marry you again in a minute!"

May your love overflow and increase for each other. . .

The Book of 1 Thessalonians

27. Write out 50 reasons you're glad to be married.

28. Be lavish with your loving words.

78. Celebrate for no reason.

*L*ight the spark of creative romance in your marriage with these 100 fabulous ideas for flirting with your spouse. Fill her sink with flowers. Wink and smile at him from across the room. Hold hands wherever you go. It's the little gestures of appreciation and gentle acts of thoughtfulness that say a great big "I love you!"

ISBN 0-7369-0390-9

9 780736 903905

HARVEST HOUSE PUBLISHERS
Eugene, Oregon 97402